Dwight Howard

SUPERSTARS IN THE WORLD OF BASKETBALL

SUPERSTARS IN THE WORLD OF BASKETBALL

Dwight Howard

Shaina Indovino

Mason Crest

Mason Crest
450 Parkway Drive, Suite D
Broomall, PA 19008
www.masoncrest.com

Printed and bound in the United States of America.

9 8 7 6 5 4 3 2

Series ISBN: 978-1-4222-3101-2
ISBN: 978-1-4222-3105-0
ebook ISBN: 978-1-4222-8795-8

Cataloging-in-Publication Data on file with the Library of Congress.

Contents

KEY ICONS TO LOOK FOR:

Text-Dependent Questions: These questions send the reader back to the text for more careful attention to the evidence presented there.

Words to Understand: These words with their easy-to-understand definitions will increase the reader's understanding of the text, while building vocabulary skills.

Series Glossary of Key Terms: This back-of-the book glossary contains terminology used throughout this series. Words found here increase the reader's ability to read and comprehend higher-level books and articles in this field.

Research Projects: Readers are pointed toward areas of further inquiry connected to each chapter. Suggestions are provided for projects that encourage deeper research and analysis.

Sidebars: This boxed material within the main text allows readers to build knowledge, gain insights, explore possibilities, and broaden their perspectives by weaving together additional information to provide realistic and holistic perspectives.

Words to Understand

versatile: Able to fill many different roles.

SETTING GOALS

Dwight runs down the court as he chases the other team. He is playing with the best players in the NBA as fans cheer in the seats above. The clock is ticking down, and it is still anybody's game. Dwight is playing on the West team in the 2013 NBA All-Star Game. This is his seventh time playing in the game, but he can't take a moment to stop and think about that. He has to stay on top of the player he is guarding at all times.

A member of the East team has reached the basket. He jumps up to take a shot. Dwight is between him and the basket. He is in perfect position to stop the shooter from scoring. He reaches up and slams the ball down and away from the basket. At almost seven feet tall, it is an easy move for Dwight. Dwight's teammate picks up the ball before it goes out of bounds and takes it back down the court. Dwight waits near the basket for the shot to be made. He blocks his opponent by getting low and spreading out his hands.

Dwight's teammate throws the ball to make a three-point shot, but he misses. The ball bounces off the rim of the basket and down toward the players below. Now is Dwight's

Dwight has become one of the most successful and popular players in the NBA, playing for the Orlando Magic and Los Angeles Lakers.

DWIGHT HOWARD

Dwight jumps for the ball at the start of a 2011 Magics game against the Golden State Warriors.

chance! He reaches up and easily grabs the ball, slamming it into the basket. His team has just scored 2 points. The game ends with the West team beating the East team by just 5 points. Dwight and his teammates scored 143 points to win the 2013 All-Star Game.

A rebound is when a player catches the ball after it has bounced off a basket or after an opponent scores. When a player stops an opponent from scoring by knocking the ball out of the way, it is known as a block. Dwight is an expert at rebounds and blocks. In fact, he scored more rebounds than any person in the 2013 All-Star Game! Dwight has also led the league in average rebounds and blocks for several years in a row.

The key to winning a game is keeping control of the ball. Players who catch a rebound are able to pass it to their teammates. In a 2006 interview, Dwight spoke about the importance of rebounds: "Rebounding is fun," he began. "I'd much rather have thirty rebounds

Growing up in Atlanta, Georgia, Dwight learned about hard work and faith from his parents, lessons he'd take with him to the NBA.

Make Connections

Dwight was born in a small town but he grew up in a large city. Children who live in the city face many challenges. Their friends might push them into trying drugs or committing crimes. Dwight said no to these pressures time and time again. Basketball was all Dwight needed to be happy. Basketball players need to be very healthy to play well. One way to stay healthy is to eat right. Another is to exercise. Athletes must also avoid putting anything in their bodies that would hurt them. This includes drugs like alcohol and tobacco. Dwight has always taken his health very seriously.

Dwight practiced abstinence, or staying away from all drugs, until he was an adult. In fact, he didn't even have his first alcoholic drink until long after he joined the NBA. One reason Dwight was able to resist drugs and crime is because his father was a state trooper. Dwight senior was a great role model because he taught Dwight not to break the law.

than thirty points. Rebounding is probably one of the toughest things you can do in the game of basketball."

EARLY LIFE

Dwight David Howard was born on December 8, 1985. He was born in the small town of Swainsboro and grew up in Atlanta, Georgia. Dwight was raised by his mother, Sheryl, and his father, also named Dwight. Both parents were serious about sports long before their son was born. Sheryl even played on a basketball team when she was in college. Her husband, Dwight Senior, became the athletic director at Southwest Atlanta Christian Academy.

Having a child was very important to Dwight's parents. They had been trying to have a child for many years before Dwight was born. There were times when the couple thought they might not be able to have children, so the Howards were overjoyed when Dwight was born. They called him a "miracle child" because of how special he was. This was long before Dwight became a popular basketball player.

Dwight learned a lot from his parents as he was growing up. One of the biggest lessons was the importance of faith. Dwight was taken to church a lot as a little kid. He learned to pray and thank God for everything he was given in life, including his basketball talent. Christians also believe in being kind to others. Dwight shows kindness both on and off the court to this day.

Kevin Garnett's skills on the court pushed Dwight to chase his own dream of playing basketball in the NBA.

Dwight Senior and Sheryl liked basketball more than any other sport. They passed this on to their son. The young Dwight was very talented with a basketball. He was very large and strong, even at a young age. His size and speed made him a great player on the court. Making baskets and dribbling the ball were easy for Dwight. He became one of the best players on any team he joined.

Dwight's skill on the court wasn't the only thing that made him popular. He also had a very good attitude about the game. Dwight did his best to help his teammates win, but having fun was most important to him. His teammates and opponents loved playing with Dwight, because he always joked around on the court. No one smiled more than Dwight when he was playing basketball.

Dwight looked up to a few basketball players while he was growing up. He loved watching Michael Jordan and Magic Johnson play, but they weren't his favorite NBA stars. Dwight found a real hero in Kevin Garnett. Kevin was large, strong, and **versatile** on the court. This meant he could fill any role where he was needed. Kevin was great at passing, stealing, and scoring. Athletes like Kevin are known as well-rounded players. Dwight wanted to be just like Kevin one day.

Many basketball players who want to join the NBA will first play in college. Playing in college helps the player get better by gaining experience. A player with more experience is more likely to be drafted. One of the reasons Dwight looked up to Kevin Garnett was because Kevin joined the NBA straight out of high school. He did not go to college, because he felt it wasn't necessary for his basketball career. Kevin was good enough to get started on his NBA career right away.

Dwight began playing basketball at the Southwest Atlanta Christian Academy (SACA) in 1998. Dwight's father worked there. The young Dwight started as a point guard. There are five positions on a basketball team. They are point guard, shooting guard, small forward, power forward, and center. Each position does something different. Some positions concentrate on shooting, while others focus on blocking.

Point guards are best at moving the ball down the court and passing it to teammates.

Dwight dreamed of playing in huge NBA arenas for cheering fans, but he'd have to work hard to make his dreams come true.

Text-Dependent Questions

1. Who won the 2013 All-Star Game? By how many points?
2. What is a rebound in basketball?
3. What role did religion play in Dwight's life? What religion did his parents teach him?
4. Where did Dwight get his love of basketball?
5. When did Dwight decide he wanted to become a professional basketball player?

They are also known as dribblers or playmakers because of how they handle the ball. If a point guard passes the ball to someone who scores, he gets an assist. Point guards help their teammates score a lot of points during a game. They may also shoot the ball if they have an opening to score.

Seventh grade was a very important school year for Dwight. It was the year he decided he wanted to become a professional basketball player. He dreamed of joining the NBA. Dwight knew being drafted wouldn't be easy. Only sixty players are drafted into the NBA each year. Dwight would have to be one of the best players entering the draft to be chosen.

Dwight wrote an essay in seventh grade about his goals in life. One of the seven goals he listed was to be chosen first in the NBA draft. To do this, he would have to be the best player in the draft. Becoming one of the best basketball players in the United States would not be easy. He would have to practice long and hard to get there. He would be more than ready by the start of the 2004 NBA draft.

Words to Understand

offensive: Trying to score.
transition: The process of changing from one thing to another.
priority: The thing you consider to be most important.

PREPARING FOR THE NBA

Dwight knew he would have to work hard to join the NBA right out of high school. This is why he joined the high school varsity team as soon as he could in 2000. Anyone who wants to join a varsity team must try out first. Varsity teams take only the best players. Dwight was good enough to make the varsity team and began the year as a small forward. Players who fill this position are very quick and skilled in all areas of basketball.

HIGH SCHOOL YEARS

High school is a great time for a basketball player to improve his skills and gain experience on the court. Dwight spent the next four years doing just that. He grew a lot between his first and second seasons on the high school varsity team. His position changed from small forward to power forward. Power forwards need to be good at both shooting and keeping opponents from taking shots.

Dwight's skill at getting the rebound after a missed shot became one of his most valuable talents when he joined the NBA years later.

Basketball statistics are recorded to keep track of how talented an athlete is. Statistics are kept in five areas: points, assists, rebounds, blocks, and steals. Dwight's statistics show just how good a rebounder he is. A rebounder can win a game, because it gives the team another shot at a basket.

Everyone on Dwight's team knew he was talented, but there was a problem. His school was so small that he wasn't getting noticed. It wasn't until Dwight's junior year that NBA and college scouts began going to his school's games to watch him play. A scout watches athletes play and decides if he will be a good fit with the team the scout represents. Dwight scored an average of 20 points and 15 rebounds a game during his junior year. The SACA team made it to the championship game with Dwight's help.

Dwight's senior year was his best yet. He averaged 25 points, 18 rebounds, and 8 blocks per game. It was clear that he was becoming a better player. The SACA team again made it to the state championships. Dwight made his family proud when the SACA basketball team won the state title in 2004.

Dwight had a great four years in high school. By the end of his senior year, Dwight was 6'11''. He scored over 2,000 points in his high school career. But his most impressive statistic was the number of rebounds he made. Dwight was great at picking up the ball after a shot. He made 1,728 rebounds in his high school years and averaged about 18 rebounds per game in his senior year. This was well above average.

Dwight earned many awards for his time spent with the SACA basketball team. He was named the Naismith and Morgan Wooten High School Player of the Year. McDonald's and Gatorade also named him National Player of the Year. Dwight was even named Mr. Basketball by the state of Georgia. It was clear by the end of Dwight's high school career that he was going to make it as a basketball player. He had finally earned the attention he deserved.

Basketball was important to Dwight, but it wasn't the only thing he cared about. He was very popular and active in his school. He even became the co-president of the student body. One of his hobbies was music, and he sang in the school choir.

Leaving high school would be a big change for Dwight. He had two options ahead of him. Either he could go straight into the NBA, or he could spend a few years in college. Going to college would let Dwight keep up with his hobbies and passions. He could play

Dwight had worked hard in high school to prove that he deserved a place in the NBA. In the 2004 NBA draft, Dwight finally had his chance to join the league.

for a college basketball team and take classes at the same time. College would also let him gain even more experience before joining the NBA. Basketball players are more likely to be picked for the NBA after they have some college experience.

Joining the NBA right away would force Dwight to leave his old life behind. NBA players who join the draft do not get to choose which team they join. Dwight would be forced to move to wherever his new team played. Basketball would take up so much of his life that he wouldn't be able to do much else. He would have to practice with his teammates during the day and rest at night. There would be no time for college classes.

THE NBA DRAFT

Dwight thought long and hard about his future. Everything he had worked for pointed toward joining the NBA straight out of high school. He always dreamed about joining the NBA. In seventh grade, he decided he would be chosen first in the NBA draft. His role model was Kevin Garnett, who had gone straight into the NBA after high school.

By June 2004, NBA scouts had been watching Dwight for years. They told Dwight he would be able to follow in Kevin Garnett's footsteps and skip college basketball. According to the sports experts, Dwight had a real shot at being chosen first in the NBA draft. This was enough to convince Dwight to sign up. He said good-bye to his high school and signed up for the June 2004 NBA draft. Each NBA team is given a chance to pick one new member from the players who sign up for the draft.

The teams with the worst record from the year before get first chance at picking new players. The team that gets to pick first will usually choose the best player in the draft. It is hoped that the talented new player will help the team get better. The NBA lottery decides the picking order. The Orlando Magic won the 2004 NBA lottery and was awarded the first pick in the NBA draft.

Dwight was excited when he found out the Orlando Magic won the draft. He knew the team needed a good *offensive* player. This meant that Dwight, a very good rebounder, would probably be the team's first pick.

Dwight was right! The Magic picked him first out of all the other players in the draft. Being picked first is a great feat for any player. It took many years of hard work, but Dwight had finally completed his goal of being the first draft pick. The only thing left to do was to create a new goal. Dwight wanted to see how far he would get in the NBA. He hoped to set some records along the way.

Dwight couldn't have been happier when he was drafted into the NBA at just 18 years old. Here, Dwight attends ESPN's ESPY Awards Show in 2004.

ROOKIE YEAR

Dwight's new team played in Orlando, Florida, which was a good location for Dwight. He was used to the weather. The city is not very far away from Atlanta, Georgia, so the drive to visit his family would not take very long.

Unfortunately, the team was not doing very well before Dwight joined. Many of its best players had left at the end of the previous season. Dwight had his work cut out for him if he was going to pave the road to victory.

Dwight chose the number 12 for his jersey. His number was partly inspired by one of the numbers Kevin Garnett used, which was 21. Dwight began the season as a starter. A starter is a player who plays at the beginning of the game and during all the important moments. Starters play more often than reserves. It is rare for a rookie—a first-year player—to be chosen as a starter.

Dwight's first year was a great one. He played in all twenty-one games that season. Dwight worked together with his new teammates to average 12 points and 10 rebounds. Scoring two digits in any two basketball categories is known as a double-double in the world of basketball. In Dwight's case, his double-double was earned through average points and rebounds.

Dwight broke a record in the 2004–2005 season, when he became the youngest player to average a double-double in the regular season. His rebounds were what brought him the most attention, though. Dwight became the youngest player to average 10 rebounds in a game. In one game, he became the youngest player to score 20 rebounds in a single game. He was ranked eighth overall for rebounds in the NBA that year.

The Orlando Magic worked very hard, and Dwight's efforts on the court were being noticed. NBA fans loved watching Dwight play. He was so fast that he would zip past opponents before they knew what happened. Fans of the Orlando Magic hoped Dwight

On the Magic, Dwight worked hard to make sure he and his team succeeded. Going from playing against high school students to playing against some of the world's best players was a big change for Dwight, but he was used to having to prove himself.

Text-Dependent Questions

1. Why was Dwight having a hard time getting noticed by the NBA when he was in high school?
2. What other things did Dwight do in high school, besides basketball?
3. Why did Dwight decide to go straight to the NBA after he graduated instead of going to college first?
4. Why did Dwight pick the number 12 for his jersey?
5. What is a double-double? How did Dwight earn his first double-double?

would be the next Shaquille O'Neal. Shaq was an amazing basketball player, who last played for the team in 1996. Like Dwight, Shaq was chosen by the Orlando Magic during the NBA draft.

Dwight was doing well in the NBA, but it was still very different from what he was used to. In 2006 Dwight was asked what it was like to join the NBA right out of high school. He said the most difficult part about the *transition* was, "Realizing that I was playing against grown men. All of a sudden I'm playing against guys who have families, are married, and here I am: eighteen, I don't have any kids, and my main *priority* is just playing and having fun." As Dwight grew older, he learned what it was like to play for a family.

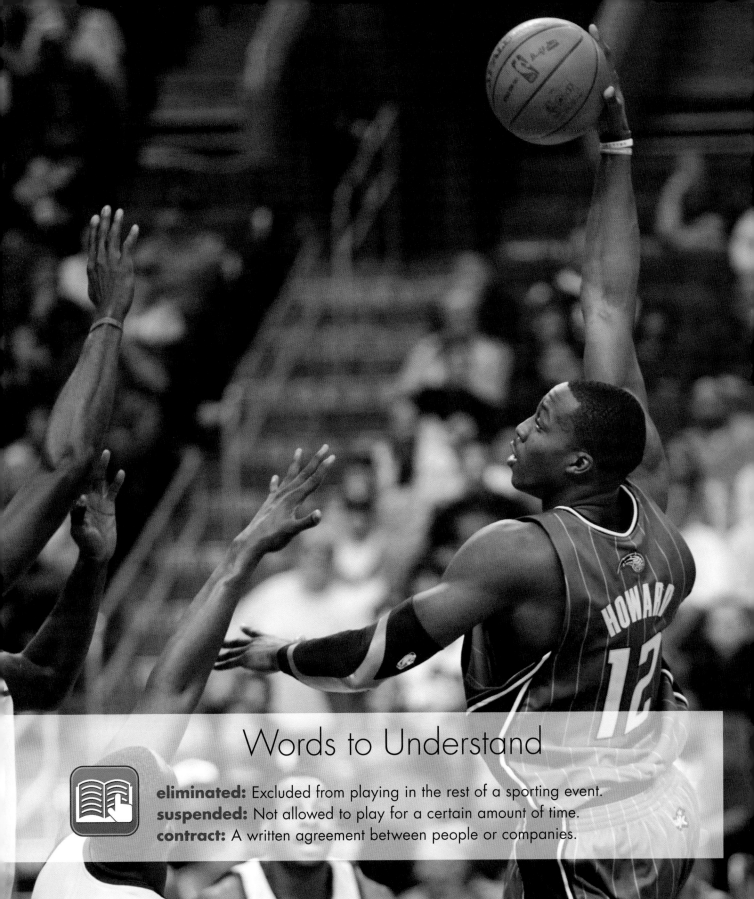

Words to Understand

eliminated: Excluded from playing in the rest of a sporting event.
suspended: Not allowed to play for a certain amount of time.
contract: A written agreement between people or companies.

The Leader in Rebounds

Dwight's second year in the NBA started off with a few changes. He had done well during his first season, but he was still thin and weak compared to other NBA players. After all, he was still just a teenager! He worked out over the summer to bulk up. All of his hard work paid off by the time the 2005–2006 season started. Dwight put on over twenty pounds of muscle during the off-season.

ORLANDO MAGIC

The Orlando Magic hired a new coach that year. His name was Brian Hill. Brian was no stranger to the Orlando Magic team. In fact, he had taken the team to the NBA finals in 1995 and the conference finals in 1996. That was when Shaquille O'Neal was still a part of the team. Brian spent a few years coaching the Vancouver Grizzlies before returning to the Magic.

After Shaq left the Magic, Dwight became the team's center. With his incredible height, Dwight was perfect for the position.

Dwight was one of the reasons the Orlando Magic chose to bring Brian Hill back to the team. Brian had trained Shaquille O'Neal. The Magic hoped Brian Hill would be able to train Dwight, too. One of the first things Brian did when he returned in 2005 was to change Dwight's position. Dwight was a lot stronger than he was his first year, and Brian believed Dwight was ready to be a center, the same position Shaq played.

Centers spend a lot of time near the basket. This position was perfect for Dwight, who liked to grab rebounds. Centers are usually very tall because they need to be able to reach the ball before opponents do. Dwight stood at an impressive 6'11''. He was more than tall enough for the position. He was also fast. He could rush down the court after retrieving the ball. Dwight was also powerful enough to smack opponents' shots away from the basket.

Brian was sure Dwight would be able to lead the Magic to the playoffs one day. But simply putting Dwight in the right position would not be enough to help the team win. Brian also needed to teach Dwight how to play better. Dwight was very talented, but he lacked experience.

Brian pushed Dwight to learn how to play better defense. This would take a while, because Dwight needed to adjust to a new playing style. Switching from one position to another is not easy if you have been playing at the same spot for many years. The 2005–2006 season started out slowly, as Dwight got used to his new role. The rest of the team was also learning how to work with a new coach.

Dwight continued breaking records in his second year. On November 15, 2005, he became the youngest player to score 20 or more points and rebounds in the same game. Toward the end of the season, he scored 28 points and 26 rebounds in a single game. He averaged over 15 points and 12 rebounds per game that season. But the Orlando Magic won only thirty-six games and did not make it to the playoffs.

The 2006–2007 season became Dwight's best season yet, and he was only in his third year. He averaged 17 points and 12 rebounds per game. During one game, he scored 35 points! He was chosen as a reserve for the 2007 NBA All-Star Game. Dwight finished the season with the most rebounds in the NBA.

This season was also a very good one for the Orlando Magic. It reached the playoffs for the first time since Dwight joined the team. They lost to the Detroit Pistons in the first round, and the Pistons went on to play in the finals. The Magic was determined to do better during the next year.

The 2007–2008 season started off with a new coach for the Magic. Coach Stan Van Gundy came to the team from the Miami Heat. Some new players were added to the team during the season, including Rashard Lewis. The Magic did well very under Stan. Dwight was chosen to join the All-Star Team again. This time, he was a starter.

The Magic made it to the playoffs in 2008. The first team the Magic faced was the Toronto Raptors. Dwight and his teammates easily beat them before moving to the next

Dwight had amazing success playing for the Magic. During his time with the team, Dwight became one of the most popular players in basketball.

round. The team's next opponent was the Detroit Pistons, the same team that **eliminated** the Magic from the playoffs the year before. The Magic lost for a second year in a row.

Dwight averaged more rebounds per game than any other player in 2008 and received a very special award for his efforts. He averaged over 14 rebounds per game that year. Winning the award was very special to Dwight, because the rebound leader of the previous four years was Kevin Garnett. Kevin was Dwight's idol when he was much younger. Now Dwight was doing even better than Kevin when it came to rebounds!

NBA FINALS

Many players are injured over the course of their careers. Dwight was exceptional. He played 351 straight games before needing to miss one in the 2008–2009 season. Dwight hurt his left knee, but he returned to the court soon after. The Magic won fifty-nine games that year. In just five short seasons, the Orlando Magic almost tripled its wins per season. The team easily qualified for the NBA playoffs once more.

The NBA playoffs went well, unlike previous years. The Magic claimed victory against many teams, including the Philadelphia 76ers and the Boston Celtics. The Orlando Magic played so well the team made it to the NBA Finals for the first time in fourteen years. This was Dwight's first time playing in the finals. He and his teammates put up a real fight against the Los Angeles Lakers but lost in the fifth game. The Lakers became the NBA champions that year.

The Magic had come so close to winning a championship. Losing in the final round was a disappointment, but Dwight had a lot to be proud of. He was named to the NBA All-Star Team for the third time and led the league in rebounds for a second year in a row. And during the 2008–2009 season, he also led the league in another statistic. He averaged more blocks per game than anyone else in the NBA.

Dwight had made himself one of the best defensive players by the end of his fifth season. He was named to the All-Defensive First Team for the first year, after being a member of the Second Team in 2008. His performance during the season also earned him the title of NBA Defensive Player of the Year. Dwight would go on to receive this title two more times.

The 2009–2010 season was much like the year before. The Magic won fifty-nine games and easily made it to the playoffs again. Dwight and his teammates defeated the Charlotte Bobcats and Atlanta Hawks to make it to the finals. The Orlando Magic and the Boston Celtics met for the championship. The Magic eliminated the Celtics the year before but could not do it again. Orlando lost in the finals for a second year in a row.

Meanwhile, Dwight continued breaking records. He became the league leader in rebounds and blocks, becoming the only player in history to win both awards two years in a row.

Dwight takes a break during the 2008 Olympics in Beijing.

Research Project

The team that Dwight was traded to in 2012, the Los Angeles Lakers, is a team with a better record in recent years than the Orlando Magic. Go online and find the team's record. How were they doing before 2012 when they got Dwight on their team? How have they done in the years since 2012? Why do you think this is?

But the next two seasons were difficult for Dwight. The Magic were not getting better. In fact, the team was getting worse. After making it to the NBA finals two years in a row, the team lost in the first round of the playoffs during the 2010–2011 season.

Dwight was not happy with the situation, and it showed on the court. He led the league in technical fouls. A foul is something that is not allowed while a game is in progress. Some fouls involve physical contact between players. Technical fouls do not involve contact. Regardless of what type of foul is made, players who commit them are punished. They are sometimes **suspended** from a game. Dwight was suspended twice that year.

Dwight's frustration was understandable. He wanted to win a championship, but it wasn't happening. The 2011–2012 season was very similar to the year before. But now Dwight's **contract** with the Magic was almost up, and he wanted to be traded. He hoped he would have a better chance winning a championship if he joined a team with a better record. His top choices were the New Jersey Nets, the Los Angeles Lakers, and the Dallas Mavericks.

If Dwight was not traded, he would become a free agent the following year. Free agents can choose to go to any team they want. If a player becomes a free agent, his previous team would get nothing in return. The Magic would lose a player and have nothing to show for it.

It took some time, but the Magic eventually decided to give Dwight what he wanted. He was traded to the Los Angeles Lakers in 2012. The Lakers had won the NBA championship against the Magic in 2009 and in 2010 against the Celtics. This made Dwight hopeful about his future.

LOS ANGELES LAKERS

Dwight was very happy when he was traded to the Los Angeles Lakers, but he didn't get to play right away. He needed to have surgery in the spring of 2012 to fix a back injury.

An advertisement tells fans about Dwight's place in the 2011 All-Star Game in Los Angeles.

Make Connections

Many of Dwight's fans were upset when he left the team. Dwight was not only one of the Magic's best players. He had also started his career with the team and helped it grow. Orlando fans and players felt betrayed when Dwight left, and they did not let Dwight forget it. In March 2013, Dwight played his first game against the Magic as a member of the Lakers. The game took place in Orlando. Dwight was fouled by members of the Magic and even booed throughout the entire game. It was clear Dwight was no longer welcome in Orlando.

Dwight was out for six months, missing most of the preseason training. So he didn't have much time to get used to playing with his new teammates before the season began.

More injuries made the 2012–2013 season difficult for Dwight. He injured his shoulder in January of 2013 and missed several more games. His rebounds per game dropped to just 12 as well. But it was still enough to make him the league leader in rebounds again. The Lakers made it to the playoffs but lost to the San Antonio Spurs in the first round. After a tough season, Dwight needed a change in his life. And soon, he'd be making another move.

Text-Dependent Questions

1. Who is Brian Hill? What other famous basketball player did he train?
2. Why was center a good position for Dwight to play?
3. What is a foul? Why did Dwight have so many of them during the 2010–2011 season?
4. Why did Dwight want to be traded away from the Magic?
5. Why didn't Dwight do as well as usual during the 2012–2013 basketball season?

Words to Understand

salary: The money you get paid each year for your job.

cultivate: Encourage or help something to grow.

DWIGHT HOWARD TODAY

Dwight had more trouble getting used to life with the Lakers than he thought he would. He was having serious health issues. Dwight knew he wasn't eating very well. His body was weak after over six months of not playing after his back surgery. He needed to work hard if he wanted to reach the same level of fitness he had during his previous seasons.

He ended his season with the Lakers as the league leader in rebounds for the fifth time. He was also selected to the All-NBA Third Team for a second time. For the seventh year in a row, Dwight became an NBA All-Star.

In an interview, Dwight said, "I want to be one of the best players in the league before I finish playing. I've got the talent and the heart and the right mindset to accomplish that goal. I know I can do it." Dwight has already proved that he can do something when he really puts his mind to it. The only thing that has held him back is his team.

Make Connections

When Dwight left the Orlando Magic, he was compared to LeBron James. Like Dwight, LeBron was the first pick of the draft the year he entered. LeBron played for the Cleveland Cavaliers for many years before deciding to join another team. His fans in Cleveland were very upset when LeBron left the Cavaliers for the Miami Heat, just like Dwight's fans in Orlando were mad when Dwight joined the Lakers. "Last year, I felt like I was the villain," Dwight said in an interview. LeBron felt the same way until he won his first championship with the Miami Heat in 2012. He regained many fans by playing well again. Dwight hopes to follow in LeBron's footsteps.

Dwight's contract with the Lakers ended after the 2012–2013 season. He became a free agent, and in July 2013, Dwight announced through his Twitter account that he would be joining the Houston Rockets. Houston finished the 2012–2013 season with 45 wins but did not get very far in the playoffs. Adding a talented center like Dwight might be enough to help the team reach the finals.

PERSONAL LIFE

Dwight has a son named Braylon. He was born on November 18, 2007. Braylon's mother is Royce Reed, who used to work for the Orlando Magic as a dancer. Dwight and Royce were once in a relationship, but they broke up after Braylon was born.

Dwight is not shy about the attention his career brings. He took part in a 2006 edition of *Extreme Makeover: Home Edition*. Dwight and a few other athletes also appeared in

Make Connections

Dwight has not become an NBA champion yet, but he has won three international medals. The first was in 2006, when Dwight played for the US basketball team during the FIBA World Championship in Japan. The United States took home the bronze medal. A year later, Dwight and his teammates won a gold medal during the 2007 FIBA Americas Championship. This competition was held in Los Vegas, Nevada. In 2008 Dwight traveled all the way to Beijing, China, to play in the Olympics. The US Olympic basketball team brought home a gold medal. Dwight was unable to play in the 2012 Olympic games, because he was recovering from surgery.

Dwight argues with a referee during a Lakers game.

Dwight has worked with shoe company Adidas to put out sneakers so fans can show their love for Dwight.

a commercial for the video game *Call of Duty: Modern Warfare 3*, which came out in 2011. Dwight has shown up in many sports magazines, including *Sports Illustrated, ESPN* magazine, and *Slam* magazine.

Dwight has had brief roles in movies, including *Just Wright* and *The Three Stooges*. His favorite movies are *Finding Nemo* and *The Lion King*. When he isn't playing basketball, Dwight likes to go bowling or practice magic tricks. In 2010 Dwight released a music album for children. It has eleven songs on it. To this day, Dwight keeps a list of his goals near his bed.

Giving young basketball fans a chance to get a good college education is important to Dwight. He's worked hard to send students to college through his scholarship.

Athletes as successful as Dwight Howard make millions of dollars each year. The more successful an athlete is, the higher his or her **salary**. Many rookies start with a low salary and work their way up to more. Most of this money is from their salary as a professional basketball player, but some of it comes from private companies. It is not uncommon for athletes to be paid by many different companies throughout the course of one season.

Many athletes have contracts with major sports companies. These contracts are known as endorsement deals. Athletes are paid a lot of money to make a brand look good. An athlete might be asked to use the brand on the court or appear in a commercial. One of

Houston is Dwight's new home while he plays for the Rockets. Dwight's future with the Rockets looks bright as he works hard to be the best player he can be.

Text-Dependent Questions

1. Why was Dwight so physically weak after 2012?
2. What is Dwight's wife's name? How did they meet?
3. What is one brand of athletic gear that Dwight has an endorsement deal with?
4. What is the D12 Foundation? What are two ways it has helped those in need?
5. How did Dwight help after the earthquake in Haiti in 2010?

the brands Dwight endorses is Adidas. He has even designed his own line of shoes that were produced by the company. Fans can buy them in stores or online.

GIVING BACK

Dwight achieved much in his career, but he will never forget his roots. When he first joined the NBA in 2004, he said he wanted to use his basketball career as a way to "raise the name of God within the league and throughout the world." Helping others is a very important part of Dwight's life and religious beliefs. He donates a lot of his money and time to good causes. In 2010 he started the D12 Foundation as a way to give back to the community that has given him so much.

The D12 Foundation site explains that Dwight's mission is, "To plant seeds, *cultivate* them, and watch them grow." Dwight tries to help the world in many ways. The first is through education. Dwight would not have been able to go as far as he did without the help of his parents and teachers. He understands that education is important for all children. D12 aims to help educate children in the United States and worldwide.

One of the ways Dwight helps education is by funding scholarships. He began the Dwight D. Howard Foundation (DDHF) to do this. Children who don't have a lot of money or resources can apply for the scholarship. The child who wins the scholarship is allowed to go to the Southwest Atlanta Christian Academy for free. The DDHF also hosts a summer camp for boys and girls. NBA players are invited to the camp to teach and inspire the children who attend.

Dwight encourages children to read as a part of the NBA's Read to Achieve program. Another way Dwight helps children is by providing food for hungry families. The D12

Foundation takes part in a coat drive that collects coats and gives them to families in need. This coat drive takes place in Orlando, where it can get cold during the winter months.

Dwight knows his popularity makes him very powerful. Many young boys and girls look up to him as one of the best basketball players in the world. This is why Dwight travels to hospitals across the country to visit sick children. He hopes meeting him will help brighten their day. For Dwight, the sky is the limit when it comes to making children feel better. He has gone to Africa and Asia to share his talent with children around the world.

When disaster strikes, Dwight is one of the first people to react. A deadly earthquake shook the island of Haiti in 2010. Many homes were destroyed, and a lot of people were killed. Dwight donated money to help rebuild the island from the ground up. This includes giving the citizens on the island a good education and great medical services. He also hopes other people will donate what they can, even if it's only a dollar. Donations can be made on the D12 website.

Dwight Howard has become one of basketball's biggest stars. Today, he's on a new team and ready to fight with them to the top of the game. Only time will show if Houston will be a good fit for Dwight. But with enough hard work, Dwight may be able to help the team snag a championship title for the first time since 1995. With big contracts, charity work, and a championship to work for, Dwight is a busy man. But Dwight's success has always come from his hard work, and today that's no different for the NBA star.

Series Glossary of Key Terms

All-Star Game: A game where the best players in the league form two teams and play each other.

Assist: A pass that leads to scoring points. The player who passes the ball before the other scores a basket gets the assist.

Center: A player, normally the tallest on the team, who tries to score close to the basket and defend against the other team's offense using his size.

Championship: A set of games between the two top teams in the NBA to see who is the best.

Court: The wooden or concrete surface where basketball is played. In the NBA, courts are 94 feet by 50 feet.

Defensive: Working to keep the other team from scoring points.

Draft (noun): The way NBA teams pick players from college or high school teams.

Foul: A move against another player that is against the rules, mostly involving a player touching another in a way that is not fair play.

Jump shot: A shot made from far from the basket (rather than under the basket) while the player is in the air.

Offensive: Working to score points against the other team.

Playoffs: Games at the end of the NBA season between the top teams in the league, ending in the Finals, in which the two top teams play each other.

Point guard: The player leading the team's offense, scoring points and setting up other players to score.

Power forward: A player who can both get in close to the basket and shoot from further away. On defense, power forwards defend against both close and far shots.

Rebound: Getting the ball back after a missed shot.

Rookie: A player in his first year in the NBA.

Scouts: People who search for new basketball players in high school or college who might one day play in the NBA.

Shooting guard: A player whose job is to take shots from far away from the basket. The shooting guard is usually the team's best long-range shooter.

Small forwards: Players whose main job is to score points close to the basket, working with the other players on the team's offense.

Steal: Take the ball from a player on the other team.

Tournament: A series of games between different teams in which the winning teams move on to play other winning teams and losing teams drop out of the competition.

Find Out More

ONLINE

D12 Foundation
www.d12foundation.org

Dwight Howard
 www.dwighthoward.com

Dwight Howard
twitter.com/DwightHoward

Houston Rockets
www.nba.com/rockets

NBA Hoop Troop
www.nbahooptroop.com

IN BOOKS

Fawaz, John. *Dwight Howard*. New York: Scholastic, 2010.

Herzog, Brad. *Hoopmania: The Book of Basketball History and Trivia*. New York: Rosen, 2003.

Peters, Stephanie, and Matt Christopher. *On the Court With . . . Dwight Howard*. New York: Little, Brown, and Co., 2010.

Savage, Jeff. *Dwight Howard*. Minneapolis, Minn.: Lerner Publications, 2011.

Schaller, Bob, and Dave Harnish. *The Everything Kids' Basketball Book: The All-Time Greats, Legendary Teams, Today's Superstars—and Tips on Playing like a Pro*. Avon, Mass.: Adams Media, 2009.

Index

About the Author

Shaina Indovino is a writer and illustrator living in Nesconset, New York. She graduated from Binghamton University, where she received degrees in sociology and English.

Picture Credits